HANDWOVEN
Baby Blankets

HANDWOVEN
Baby Blankets

TOM KNISELY

STACKPOLE
BOOKS

Published by
STACKPOLE BOOKS
4501 Forbes Boulevard, Suite 200
Lanham, Maryland 20706
www.stackpolebooks.com

Distributed by NATIONAL BOOK NETWORK

First edition

Cover design by Wendy A. Reynolds
Photography by Kathleen Eckhaus

Library of Congress Cataloging-in-Publication Data

Knisely, Tom.
  Handwoven baby blankets / Tom Knisely. — First edition.
     pages   cm
  Includes bibliographical references.
  ISBN 978-0-8117-1411-2
     1. Hand weaving—Patterns. 2. Blankets. 3. Infants'
supplies. I. Title.

  TT848.K59 2015
  746.1'4—dc23

                          2015019474

Printed in India

This book is dedicated to my granddaughter, Windsor Sara Bixler. You came into my life during unsettling times. You righted my sails and steadied this old ship during the storm and I am forever grateful. You slowed me down and moved me in new directions and have taken me places that I would have never ventured. Thank you, Windsor. I believe that God, the Universe, or something larger and greater than myself brought you to me at just the right time. I stand in awe and ponder how this all works.

Take my hand, little Windsor . . . we have a long journey to travel together and I have a lot to show and teach you.

Contents

INTRODUCTION

Oh, Baby!

Windsor Sara Bixler

It's instinctive to wrap a baby in a nice warm baby blanket, don't you think?

I remember it like it was yesterday. When my children were born, the nurses cleaned the girls up and wrapped them tightly in warm pink cotton blankets. What a thrill to see them! (When I think back on it now, each time it was sort of like holding a "grande" pink burrito with the most beautiful little face coming out from the end.)

"Is she all right?" I would ask the nurse. "This blanket seems a little tight and she can't move much," I said.

The attending nurse would reassure me that she was indeed fine and to think for a moment where the baby had been for the past forty weeks. Not exactly a spacious park! Of course, the nurse was right. Our baby was content and seemed perfectly happy to be put back into a small, warm environment.

So flash forward several years.

When I heard that my daughter Sara and her husband Dustin where expecting, I decided to make them a baby blanket. This is just what a weaver does, right? Well, commitments of work and writing my first book on rag rugs interfered. The weeks passed and soon we were presented with a beautiful granddaughter named Windsor.

So here I am with stacks of rag rugs woven for the book—and no baby blanket. Well, did I feel terrible? Of course I did. But I reminded myself that not every child born has a relative that weaves. Fortunately, Miss Windsor was gifted a number of beautiful blankets that blurred the fact that her grandfather had not woven her a special blanket of his own. And besides, there will be plenty of time to weave a blanket for Windsor. Maybe a blanket better suited for a toddler, or a blanket for an older child who wants to cuddle up with someone he or she loves for story time.

Blankets aren't just for babies. Lots of children would love a special blanket to call their own, especially if they are going through a rough time. What better gift could you give a child going through a frightening time than your love, a stuffed toy, and a beautiful cozy blanket?

In the following pages you'll find a number of different blankets that I designed to give you inspiration to weave a blanket for that special tiny someone. These pattern drafts range from beginning level to intermediate, and all the way up to designs for the advanced weaver. There are threading drafts for 4 and 8 shafts. There are simple, plain weave blankets; twill blankets; and blankets using more complex structures, such as overshot, summer and winter, and lace weaves.

The baby and parents may not be impressed or have any idea what effort you put into weaving a blanket, even if they love the result. But the process might as well be interesting and fun for you, right?

Take a look at the designs and be inspired. Change them around and make the designs yours. Substitute threads to make changes that better suit the needs of the child or parents. A heavy wool blanket may not be appreciated in a warm climate, so make a southern baby a blanket in cotton. Or if you love that cotton blanket but really want a blanket for a baby way up north, switch it over to wool. You are the weaver and you know what is best.

I hope you find some ideas that excite you. Baby blankets are fun to weave—colorful, soft, and quick. In many ways, they are the perfect project for the hand weaver.

And now, it's off to the loom!

PART 1

The Basics

- Size

- Colors

- Materials

- Finishes

CHAPTER 1

How Large? How Small?

Guess what? There is no definitive answer to this question. A quick Internet search brought some surprising results. One experts suggested that for a preemie, a blanket should be about 18" square. This to me seems more like a kitchen towel and a preemie will soon outgrow such a small blanket. Another suggestion was for approximately 48" by 60". That to me seems a little large and more like a lap throw for Grandma.

There are so many different ideas on this that I decided to go through the stacks of baby blankets that we have here in the house. These included the blankets that my daughters had as children and my new granddaughter's baby blankets. Most of them are around 30" to 36" square. Some of the blankets were rectangular (30" x 48").

Now some of these blankets are knitted, some crocheted, some quilted, and some handwoven. I discovered that the blankets that were used the most and took the biggest beating from love and wear from the little ones were those that were a little larger. They had lasted through my daughters' toddler years and probably were used for all sorts of things, like playing house, making forts, and who knows what else. This larger size makes perfect sense to me.

When designing these baby blankets I took two things into consideration. First of all, I considered my blanket research project; and secondly, I thought about the weaving width of many looms. As you know, the weaving width is the actual width that can be warped onto a loom without distorting the threads. You can determine the weaving width of your loom by measuring the harness frame's open area. (Measure the area where the warp is threaded and passes through the harness frame, not the outside of the frame. Please do not measure the beater's frame—that measurement may be up to 12" wider than the real weaving width.)

Many loom manufacturers follow this basic guide to making looms. They offer floor looms with weaving widths of 36", 45", and 60". Manufacturers also make looms with smaller weaving widths that are intended to be portable, but these are not the looms that we would generally weave a blanket on anyway. So what you'll find in these projects are blanket drafts of 32" to 36" in the reed. This should accommodate most looms and most weavers.

When designing and weaving your own designs, or adapting one of mine from the book, the real answer to the question "How large is a baby blanket?" is that it is up to you.

Warp it as wide as you like and weave it as long as you like. Remember, as with all weaving, there is take-up and draw-in as you weave. Allow for about 10% to 15% for each in the blanket designs in this book.

Whatever you decide, remember that no size is really wrong. It all depends on you and the baby you are weaving for. A handwoven baby blanket will be loved and treasured by the parents and the babe.

A WORD ON HEDDLES

Before we go any farther: COUNT YOUR HEDDLES! First of all, there is nothing more frustrating than getting close to the end of your threading and finding out that you have run out of heddles on a harness frame. Especially if that harness frame is toward the interior of the castle of your loom, like harness

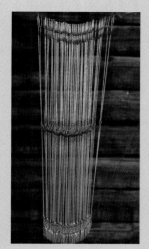

frame #5. You will have to work through all the rest of the frames just to add a few heddles. It's possible to do, but it is not enjoyable.

The other problem that you might encounter is too many heddles left on the harness frame after you have completed your threading. A large number of unused heddles pushed to the side of a harness frame will distort the edge threads in your warp and cause tension problems. Remember, your edge threads should pass through the harness frames as smoothly as the rest of warp; they should never have to bend and stretch around a bunched up group of unthreaded heddles.

Too many heddles? Here's what you do.

Solution #1: Remove the extra heddles.

If you purchased your loom brand new from the manufacturer you might recall that the heddles came on a large loop of string. The string passed through the top portion of the heddles and looped around and back through the bottom portion of the heddles, and then the two ends where tied in a knot. This keeps the heddles in order. The part of the heddle that the string goes through is the part that slides onto the heddle bars on the harness frame. If you want to remove heddles from the harness frame it's not difficult. Take a strong piece of thread such as 8/4 cotton carpet warp, 24" to 30" long, and thread the end onto a tapestry needle or bodkin. Count out the number of heddles you want to remove and slide them toward the side of the harness frame where you want to slip them off. Take the needle or bodkin and pass the tip between the smooth surface of the heddle bar and the loop of metal that makes up the top of the heddle. Push the needle along, making sure that each heddle is being threaded onto the string. When you have threaded the top of the heddles, bring the needle down to the bottom and return back the way you came, repeating the same threading operation. Be very careful not to pull the end of the string out of the top! The two ends of

the string can now be tied together. Now carefully remove the bottom heddle bar from the side of the harness frame and slide the unwanted heddles off the end of the heddle bar. Replace the heddle bar immediately. Then do the same for the top heddle bar.

There you go—you now have plenty of room for the warp to pass through the harness frame. Repeat the same operation for any of the other harness frames.

Solution #2: Distribute the extra heddles.

There is an alternative technique. You can store the unwanted heddles in between the threaded heddles. You do this as you are threading the loom. Here is an example that is easy to follow. Let's say you are threading a blanket that is going to be 36" wide in the reed and the loom has a 36" weaving width. Most likely the maker of your loom has provided a little wiggle room in regard to the opening in the width of your harness frame. If the open area of your harness frame is 36.5" or 37", that is not a lot of extra space to store your unused heddles. If the warp is set at 12 epi and is 36" wide, than you have a total of 432 threads. If you are threading a straight draw twill (1, 2, 3, 4), you will need to thread 108 heddles on each of the four harness frames. If your loom has 200 heddles on each harness frame, you would have a total of 92 unthreaded or unused heddles at the edge of your harnesses and this will distort the natural flow of the warp. So here is what you do: Thread the first four heddles, one on each harness frame, and then slip an empty heddle over on each of the frames. Continue this way all across the threading of the warp. As you get close to the end of the threading, be sure to count and leave enough heddles on each harness to complete the threading. This will distribute the heddles evenly on the frames and the unthreaded heddles will easily ride up and down on the frames as if they were pushed to the side.

This trick is much easier than removing your heddles and then having to put them back onto the frames later.

Planning ahead pays off in the end. So count those heddles!

CHAPTER 2

What Colors Shall I Use?

Pink for girls and blue for boys? Or something non-traditional and a little edgy?

Shopping for a newborn or toddler these days can be daunting. There is so much to choose from. The one thing that it seems has not changed is that blue is for boys and pink is for girls, the time-honored means of gender identification. Years before sonograms and amniocentesis, families patiently waited nine months to see what gender the baby was. People who wanted to get a head start buying clothes and accessories usually picked colors that were gender neutral, such as yellow and green. Today many couples know the sex of their child long before that baby arrives.

If you are wondering what colors capture a newborn baby's attention, don't spend time worrying about it. Modern research tells us a newborn can focus only about 12 to 18 inches away and what they see best are strong contrasts of black, grays, and white. They notice strong patterns, such as checks and plaids. By two to three months, Baby will able to see different colors. Red comes first, and then blue and yellow. A few months later Junior will finally be able to recognize the difference between red and orange or blue and green.

I can remember my daughter's arms and legs going when the mobile over the crib was turned on and the brightly colored animals moved to a tinny sounding lullaby. (Now that I think about it, was she kicking and flailing her arms with joy? Or was she begging me to please turn that mobile off because it was getting on her nerves and she just wanted to go to sleep?) As a doting daddy, I stood there and pressed the button over and over to make it go around and around, and I stood there thinking she loved it.

Today it seems that any color or combination of colors are baby colors. After all, the baby really doesn't care what color the nursery is as long as it is soft and smells right. Yes, smells right. One of my students told me that her two-year-old son was upset because she washed his blanket and took all the good smells out of it. He couldn't care less about the blanket's color, but he sure missed that smell that he loved. A baby blanket should appeal to all the senses.

The colors I chose for these blankets were strictly of my own liking. They are colors I thought would look good together. Since these are fabrics designed for baby, I wanted them to stimulate and attract a little baby's attention. I used contrasting colors when combining several colors together, but I also wove some blankets as monochromatics. Both approaches make wonderful baby blankets.

Sometimes you just want to weave a blue blanket. Or a pink one. By using different values of a single color, that is, lights and darks or tints and shades of blue, you will weave a baby blanket that is satisfying. Monochromatic projects are exciting in their own way.

I also used hand-dyed and variegated yarns in this collection. Here is a tip to remember: when you warp and weave with variegated yarns, the subtle color changes that move though the length of the yarn create effects in the finished fabric and often lead to unexpected patterning, sometimes a patterning that is a complete surprise. I have even used variegated yarns in both the warp and weft and found I wove fabric looking like a tartan plaid.

If you are using hand-dyed yarns be sure you have enough to complete the blanket. Reproducing a special hand-dyed yarn is nearly impossible. When winding the warp with these variegated and hand-dyed yarns remember to leave a few yards in case you break a warp thread or two. You will be so glad you did.

Have fun with your color choices, but don't agonize over the decision; I know you want the blanket to be absolutely perfect for this baby, but the truth of the matter is there are no wrong color choices. We are limited by the color selection offered by the yarn industry and this makes picking colors a bit more difficult sometimes. You might need to rethink your thread choice and choose a different type of yarn.

WEAVING WITH VARIEGATED FIBERS

The length of the color run in a variegated yarn can give you a clue as to the end result. Do the colors change every few inches along the length of the thread? Or does the color continue for several yards before moving into the next color? A yarn with long runs of color will weave into weft-way stripes: if your warp is only 30" to 36" wide on the loom and your weft yarn has a color run of 4 yards in length before it changes, you will get stripes because you might have several passes of the shuttle before the color changes. Isn't this fun to think about?

I have woven many projects with variegated or hand-dyed yarns and I still learn something from each project. For instance, the width of the warp in the reed can change the color patterning. A difference of 1" in the width will shift where the colors fall, and you would swear you were weaving with a different thread. You can't really plan for this: the process is completely serendipitous.

One width in the reed may give you a subtle movement of stripes; a slightly wider or narrower width may cause color pooling, concentrating a color in one spot. If you're lucky, the color blotch will resemble a Mr. Moon or a sweet kitty. If for some freaky reason the color blotch you've woven resembles creepy old Uncle Albert, STOP! Simply unweave back to the beginning and remove a few threads at the selvedge edges to make the blanket a little narrower. Then pull out the unwanted threads from the reed and heddles, toss them off the back of the loom, and start weaving again. Your blanket will look completely different.

Now go have a nice cup of tea to celebrate that you noticed the problem in time to fix it!

In this sampler, the width of the warp is the only variable; I used the same variegated weft throughout. The results are very different—and all due to the warp width.

CHAPTER 3

What Materials Are Best for Baby?

When it comes to picking out the threads for your baby blanket, you want to be mindful of the baby's delicate skin. Choose a yarn that is soft to the touch but strong enough to hold up to the physical action of weaving. A soft feeling yarn might not hold up as warp, but would be fine as your weft.

Knitting yarns and weaving yarns are sometimes very different in their construction. The materials used and the amount of twist in a thread can vastly change the appearance and feel of that yarn in your hand and ultimately the finished blanket.

Here is a story about using a very unlikely thread for a baby blanket. Your weaving instructors and mentors will tell you the best way to see how a thread works is to weave a sample. But nobody I know likes to weave a sample, including me. I usually wait to the end of a warp and then if I have some remaining warp left I will weave a sample of something that has inspired me.

As many of you know I am primarily known as a rug weaver. After teaching a workshop on weaving rag rugs, one of the looms had quite a bit of yardage left to be woven off. The loom was warped with 8/4 cotton carpet warp and had a sett of 12 epi (ends per inch). I retied the warp and wove the rest of the warp with 8/4 cotton instead of using the rags we used in class. I beat it to square with 12 ppi (picks per inch). I washed the fabric on a regular cycle in the washer and then threw it in the dryer. Much to my amazement, the fabric was wonderful and had a softness and hand that was perfect for a baby blanket!

Now, who would have thought that cotton carpet warp would be a good candidate for weaving a baby blanket. But it turned out to be perfect and—best of all—it comes in dozens of beautiful colors. So that's the lesson here: sampling is a good thing. (I still really don't like to do it, but remember that you sometimes need to sample an unlikely yarn or thread to see what the possibilities are.) Carpet warp is a thread that I was very familiar with, but had I not woven that quick little sample, I never would have discovered this very different application.

My daughter and son-in-law blessed me with a beautiful granddaughter. My granddaughter, of course, doesn't have

much to say as to what blanket mommy or daddy wraps her in. But it has been interesting to watch which blankets my daughter goes to first or grabs quickly as they go out the door. My granddaughter was born in the summer so her first blankets were cotton and lightweight. When fall came around, the blankets became a little heavier but still were cotton or a cotton blend. These blankets are a favorite because they can be easily washed and dried in the dryer.

So this is what I learned in my very own home, watching my granddaughter and her parents. The favorite blankets were mostly based on three things. First, the weight of the blanket in relation to the weather. Lightweight in the summer and heavier weight blankets in the cool of the autumn

and winter. It goes without saying that all of the blankets were soft to the touch.

The second factor was the colors in the blanket. My daughter Sara is an artist and very aware of color and color combinations. She knows what she likes and is not afraid to step out of the boundaries of the pink-and-blue way of thinking. The third factor was ease of laundering. Choose fibers that will be easy to wash and dry and hold up well to frequent laundering.

These little observations were invaluable as I planned this book. Each design needed to be woven with materials that are easily obtainable, with a nice soft feel in the woven piece, and must be a breeze to care for. So the blanket designs in this book use cotton, cotton blends, and some wool blends. A baby blanket woven from wool yarns that are handspun, hand dyed, and from a sheep named Fluffy would be very attractive to have. But these special baby blankets are best for very special occasions, probably not everyday use. If practicality is important, then plan a wash-and-wear blanket. The care and laundering of a baby blanket should be one of the first things to think about as you choose your yarns.

Two blankets in this collection were woven with white cotton and white rayon threads, designed for very special

occasions, perhaps a christening or a baby's naming ceremony. These blankets look fancy and special, but the truth of the matter is these blankets can also be used every day because the materials used to weave them are easy to launder.

It is important to help the baby's parents understand this so that they use the blanket and don't put it away for safekeeping. Tell them a blanket is meant to be used—it is durable and it is washable. And if in a few years the precious blanket looks a little tired and worn, you will be happy to weave the child another one.

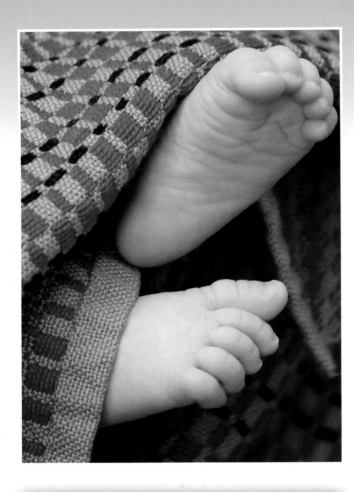

CHAPTER 4

Finishing Your Baby Blanket

■ WASHING WOOL BLANKETS

Wool yarns are a little more finicky than cotton. I sometimes hand wash a wool blanket or wash it on a delicate cycle. Then I either lay it out and air dry the blanket or put it into the dryer and set the dryer for air fluff. You don't want to risk felting it. There are many superwash wool yarns on the market, treated to be machine washable. They will not felt when washed and dried in the dryer. Add a little hair conditioner to the rinse water—that will greatly improve the hand of the wool blanket. Wool is a protein-based fiber, so the wool used for your blanket is protein, as is the hair on your head. A little hair conditioner does wonders for the blankets. Try it on your wool sweaters the next time you wash them. An inexpensive hair conditioner is all you need.

You're now ready to get started on your baby blanket. But it is important to think about the last steps before you even throw the first shuttle. So let's talk about finishing.

There are many ways to finish a piece and you don't want to limit your options because of something you did in the beginning. Here is a good example—you can learn from my mistakes. In my early days of weaving I decided to weave a set of placemats that would have a 1" knotted fringe on each end. As I wove the placemats I put a 2" spacer between each placemat. "This will give me 1" on each end of the placemat," I thought. "When I am finished weaving and take them off the loom I will simply cut between the placemats and tie the knots."

Can you see the error of my ways? I am embarrassed to tell you that I didn't realize my dilemma until I sat down at the table to cut and tie the knots. There was no way that my chubby fingers could manipulate that short length of fringe into a secure knot. The only option was to run the placemats under the sewing machine to hem them. I had no choice. Now I leave a minimum of 5" to 6" of warp to make knotted fringe, and then trim the ends to the length I want. Think about the finish before you even begin!

Finishing is a two-step process. The first step is to secure the beginning and ending edges so that the woven area doesn't start to unweave itself. The second step is to wash the fabric, a process called wet finishing. When newly woven fabric is placed in warm soapy water, the threads become limp, which allows them to snuggle in around themselves, interlocking more closely and making the fabric more stable.

You're not washing the fabric because it's dirty; wet finishing improves the hand and feel of the blanket. And often washing helps to improve the selvedges and even out the beat lines. It never ceases to amaze me how a length of fabric that I have woven transforms itself from a rough and sometimes scratchy surface to a soft and supple hand by simply wet finishing. (When working with wool, we call this fulling the fabric.)

For a baby blanket the most practical finish is a simple rolled hem. This not only eliminates the fringe becoming a choking hazard, it makes the blanket easy to wash. A fringed edge may look beautiful on something that is meant to be decorative but loses its practicality on a blanket that will be washed frequently. Fringes get tangled in the wash and need to be combed out, and in the case of a cotton warp, the short length of the cotton fiber makes fringe disintegrate after several washings.

So weavers, the final word on this subject is NO FRINGE! A simple rolled hem is the best way to finish your blanket.

You can sew a commercial binding along the edge of your blanket. To some weavers, a satin binding sewn onto the edge of a handwoven blanket goes against all the rules of being truly handwoven—they swear that there is an unwritten rule that everything about their project must be done by hand, from measuring the warp and threading the loom to rolling the hem and sewing it by hand. But let's be realistic for a moment. Babies love that silky feel of a satin binding. Picture a baby with a thumb in her mouth and the other hand rubbing the edge of the blanket between her little thumb and fingers—babies love silky edges. So go for it. It's all about the baby anyway, right? And there is no need to sew it on by hand—sew it on by machine if you prefer.

Ok, here goes: there is nothing wrong with a crocheted edge on a handwoven baby blanket. There, I said it. I don't know why I had such opposition to crocheted edgings on blankets, but I did. In my mind there are all kinds of baby blankets: knitted, crochet, woven, quilted . . . who knows how many more? So why can't we cross over and use two mediums in the same piece? A crocheted edging is an eye-catching treatment for a blanket. It can cover up a rough-looking selvedge as it frames the blanket.

Take a look at the edge of the blanket I called Rainbow. The crocheted edge is perfect on this blanket. The weft yarn was slubby with thick and thin areas; it is impossible to achieve an even selvedge with these yarns. So cover those uneven edges with crochet. By using the same yarn as the weft or a solid colored yarn that matches one of the colors in the blanket, you have a clever, functional finish.

The second phase of the finish requires washing the blanket, or wet finishing. If you are an experienced weaver and have washed other handwoven projects you know the impor-

tance of wet finishing. If you are new to weaving, I promise you that you will be totally surprised with the finished results. Washing your handwoven blanket will bring all those threads together and meld them into one glorious piece of fabric. Don't be afraid to throw your blanket in the wash. Baby blankets need to be washable anyway, and since you have chosen yarns that are machine washable there is no need to worry.

Single crochet edging using the same yarn as was used in the warp. Tip: serge or zigzag the fringe end and trim with a rotary cutter before crocheting.

Cotton and cotton blends are the easiest to machine wash. Warm water and a mild soap will do nicely. All of the blankets in this book were machine washed and dried. The cotton and cotton blends and the Tencel blankets all had a little fabric softener added to the wash water. You will be surprised how a baby blanket woven from cotton carpet warp will transform into such soft fabric with the addition of fabric softener. Use the unscented softeners if you object to the strong fragrance of some softeners.

Finishing your blanket is not difficult, but it is important to think ahead. How do you want to finish this blanket? Figure that out even before you wind the warp. I promise you that you will be glad you did.

CHAPTER 5

A Word About The Projects

*I*f you would have told me a few years ago that I would be writing a book about baby blankets I would have said you were crazy. I was far too busy to write a book and why would I write about baby blankets, anyway? I would have told you that teaching and rug weaving are my passions. Well, here we are a few years later. I am still teaching people how to weave, from beginning weaving classes to more advanced classes, and I now have written my first book on rag rugs.

So now I'm writing about baby blankets. Having Windsor in my life, I'm well aware of all things baby. But it is more than that. I wanted this book to be more than just a book of weaving patterns for small little blankets. I wanted this book to be a lesson book about color and textures and I want it to introduce you to weave structures that you may be aware of but have never woven before. This book is as much for you, the weaver at the loom, as it is for that sweet little baby that the blanket is intended for.

I wanted to design blankets for every weaver out there. There is always something new to learn, whether you are a brand new weaver or an experienced weaver. Experienced weavers may be reintroduced to a weave structure that they used for dish towels years before; here it is as a baby blanket, and suddenly you might remember how much you enjoyed weaving that pattern.

I hope you like the pattern drafts and will try several of them. It's good to have a stash on hand for that unexpected shower that you get invited to. You know there will be more babies in your life. If you plan ahead, you can go the closet

and pull out a beautiful handwoven baby blanket—what a great gift!

The pattern drafts here are intended to be an inspiration. You can follow them exactly as they are written and woven or you can change them to make them more personal. And of course, colors are such a personal choice—feel free to change anything so that it pleases you and the parents. Remember, baby doesn't care.

I have written this book so that the patterns will be just as fresh and in style in twenty or thirty years. I have pattern books on my personal shelf that are sixty years old and are still as exciting as the day they were first published. And sadly, some books are not that exciting. I am telling you this because some of the older books on my book shelf recommend threads that have not been available for years. The

A WORD ON THE WARP LENGTH

For the blankets in this book, a warp of 2½ yards will be enough for one blanket. If you intend to weave 2 blankets, make the warp 4 yards long. We wove many of the blankets somewhere between 48" and 55" long. This length allowed for a rolled hem and allowed for the take-up shrinkage from the first washing during the finishing process.

solution is to find something comparable to the threads the pattern calls for. Don't be afraid to make changes, and if you are doubting your choice of threads or color choice, weave a sample. No one likes to weave them but they tell so much about your choice of threads.

I have given you typical important information regarding the warping and weaving of your blanket. In most cases, I have purposely left out the warp length. Some of you will weave just one blanket and some might decide to weave two or three on the same warp. By changing out the weft colors you can weave several blankets that look vastly different on the same warp. I did this with the blanket I called Pretty in Pink. I planned this warp as blankets for twin girls. The warp is pink and white stripes, giving the weaver lots of options. One blanket is woven with only a pink weft, and the other is woven with white weft. The blankets are related but they look quite different. For triplets, I could have made the warp even longer and woven the third blanket as a check, with pink and white stripes woven horizontally. Can you see the efficiency in warping a longer warp and weaving several blankets? You are threading and sleying the reed, anyway—just wind on a little more warp and you are ready to weave a second (or third or fourth) blanket.

In my opinion, it is important to complete a pattern repeat in the blanket. If the blanket is a little longer than you expected, that is better than stopping mid-pattern just because you reached a certain length based on some arbitrary instructions. And try to keep your blanket's length in proportion to the width. Remember that the baby isn't going to mind one bit if it is a little short, and the parents aren't going to know that you ran out of thread 3" from your intended goal!

Relax and enjoy your weaving. Oh, and before I forget, congratulations on your new baby!

■ TOM'S FAVORITE HEM

I don't know who to credit for this hem-marking idea. I have been using it myself and teaching it to students in one form or another for years.

The idea of weaving doubled weft rows goes against my better judgment. We all know that this is technically incorrect, because if you weave a double weft row you're weaving a flaw into the fabric. But this wonderful little intentionally woven flaw at the ends of your woven piece can help greatly when you are making an even rolled hem.

The advantage comes because with this "flaw" you will see that you are weaving a subtle straight horizontal line that becomes your fold line. By weaving the double lines at different widths you reduce the chances of having bulk in the hem.

Try weaving a sample of this hem first on a warp that's left over from another project. Remove it from the loom and take it to the ironing board, fold the fabric on the doubled lines, and press it with a steam iron. The fold will turn easily and you will be able to see the hem line more clearly than than if you try to fold and hem without the lines.

Here are two examples for your consideration. One is for a plain weave hem and the other is for a twill. I think you will like what you see and use this again and again on your projects.

PLAIN WEAVE HEM

TWILL HEM

PART 2

The Blankets

- 4-Shaft Patterns
- 8-Shaft Patterns

Pretty in Pink

This is a very simple blanket to weave, and yet look how pretty it is with classic bold stripes of natural and rose running the length of the blanket. For twin girls, it is easy to weave two that are related and yet as different and individual as the babies you're weaving them for. Weave the first blanket with only natural in the weft and weave the second blanket with a rose weft. Or weave a checkerboard pattern by alternating rose and natural colored stripes in the weft.

PRETTY IN PINK

Threading draft

4				4				4				4				4			
	3				3				3				3				3		
		2				2				2				2				2	
			1				1				1				1				1

(6x)	(3x)	(6x)	(3x)	(6x)
Balance	←	5x		→

	4
3	
	2
1	

Treadling

1		
	1	4x
	1	6x — Hem
1		8x
1		
	1	8x
1		
	1	
1		Body of Blanket
	1	
1		
	1	
1		8x
	1	
	1	6x — Hem
1		
1		4x
	1	

4-SHAFT PLAIN WEAVE

Warp: 4/2 cotton
Colors:
- ▓ Rose, 204 ends
- ░ Natural, 180 ends

Sett: 12 epi

Width in reed: 32"

Warp length:
For two blankets: 4 yds.
For one blanket: 2.5 yds.

Weft: Same as warp
Colors:
- ▓ Rose (Blanket 1)
- ░ Natural (Blanket 2)

Irish Meadows

*I*nspiration can come knocking at the door almost any time, sometimes when it's least expected and not always at a convenient moment. Such was the case of this pattern that I call Irish Meadows. At a wedding I noticed a gentleman wearing a great Harris Tweed jacket. And there, sitting just a few pews up from me, was a striking broken twill that used multiple colors in the warp. Snap! What a great idea. I can use that idea in my weaving, I thought. And here it is.

IRISH MEADOWS

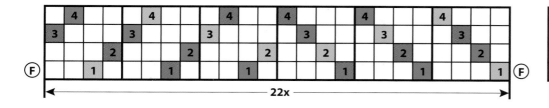

←———————— 22x ————————→

4-SHAFT BROKEN TWILL

Warp: 8/4 cotton carpet warp
   Colors:

      Colonial Green, 176 ends

      Dark Green, 176 ends

      Olive Green, 176 ends

Sett: 16 epi

Width in reed: 33"

Warp Length: 2.5 yds.

Weft: 8/4 cotton carpet warp
   Color:

      Lime Green

Note: Ⓕ denotes floating selvedge. I used Lime Green.

Tutti Frutti

This is one of my favorite basket weave structures because it has a plain weave frame surrounding the basket weave squares. This makes it a little more stable than a conventional basket weave. Use a solid color for the threads that frame the baskets to make the design pop. And try this threading sometime for dish towels using finer unmercerized cotton threads.

TUTTI FRUTTI

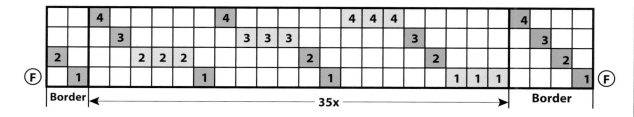

4-SHAFT BASKET WEAVE

Warp: 8/2 cotton
  Colors:

    Sherbet (variegated), 420 ends

    Turquoise, 286 ends

Sett: 20 epi

Width in reed: 35.5"

Warp length: 2.5 yds.

Weft: 8/2 cotton
  Colors:

    Sherbet (variegated)

    Turquoise

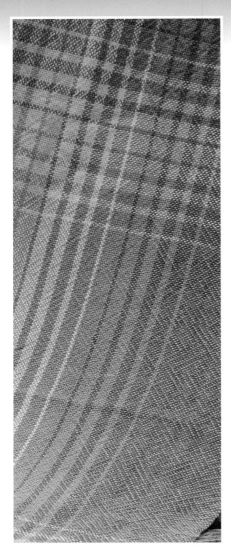

springtime

*J*ust look how cheerful this blanket is. The bright colors that we associate with spring make for a very pretty blanket. The colors in the stripes slowly change from one into another, giving the design a soft look. We wove this blanket two ways so you could see how different the blankets could be. One was woven with a solid colored weft; the second blanket was woven by squaring the colors in the warp arrangement. How about putting on an extra long warp and weaving several blankets using the other colors from the warp as a single color weft? Try a textured thread in a cheerful color or a variegated yarn from your local knitting shop. The possibilities are endless and the weaving is so much fun.

SPRINGTIME

4-SHAFT PLAIN WEAVE

Warp: 8/4 cotton carpet warp
Colors:

- Purple, 60 ends
- Moody Blue, 100 ends
- Grass Green, 100 ends
- Pear, 100 ends
- Coral, 50 ends

Sett: 12 epi

Width in reed: 34.2"

Warp length:
2.5 yds. for one blanket
4 yds. for two blankets

Weft: 8/4 cotton carpet warp
Blanket #1:

- Grass Green

Blanket #2:
Weave squaring the colors in a "Tromp as Writ" order.

The original version is woven with weft colors that mirror the warp colors. This one is woven with just green.

Reverse from center

Color Draft

Threading

			4
		3	
	2		
1			

	1		1		1		1		1		1		1		1		1		3	
1			1	1		1		1		1		1			1	1		2		4
4x		**6x**		**8x**		Body of blanket: weave to length				**8x**		**6x**		**4x**						
Hem										**Hem**										

Carson's Blanket

During the writing of the book we found out that my editor's son and his wife were expecting their first child. You know what they say about timing? So I designed a blanket for Zach's new baby. The yarn I chose is a sock yarn spun from soft wool and nylon. Sometimes you reject the idea of wool for a baby blanket, but this yarn is spun specifically for socks that you throw into the washing machine and dryer. So why not use this beautiful yarn for a baby blanket? As you can see, it works just fine.

4-SHAFT ROSE PATH TWILL

Warp: Trekking (XXL) Sock Yarn
   Color: Variegated

Sett: 16 epi

Width in reed: 34"

Warp length: 5.5 yards for three blankets

Weft:
   Blanket #1: Same as warp

   Blanket #2: Burgundy

   Blanket #3: Teal

CARSON'S BLANKET

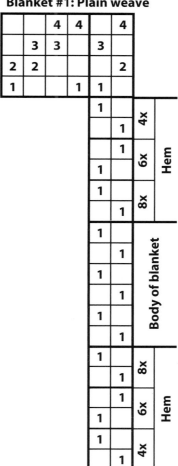

Blanket #1: Plain weave

Hem

Body of blanket

Hem

Blanket #2: Twill, use twill hem

Body of blanket

Blanket #3: Rose path twill, use twill hem

Body of blanket

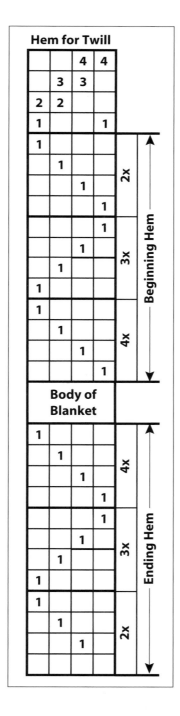

Hem for Twill

Beginning Hem

Body of Blanket

Ending Hem

A Tartan for Scotty McGee

This blanket is woven from Jagger Spun yarns and is 100% Merino wool. People sometimes shy away from wool because it's scratchy. Well, not this blanket; it is woven from some of the softest wool threads known. You will have to hand wash this blanket and let it air dry to prevent felting and shrinkage. Don't be afraid to use it, though. It will hold up and be loved for years. The bright colors will appeal to a little one and so I designed it in a tartan plaid arrangement. After weaving, it was washed in warm water with a gentle soap. Squeeze excess water out by hand or spin it in the washer. Then soak it in warm water again with hair conditioner, 20 to 30 minutes, to soften the fibers. Then squeeze it out again and rinse it in warm water. Air dry your blanket. A commercial satin binding can make a nice finish.

A TARTAN FOR SCOTTY MCGEE

Color draft

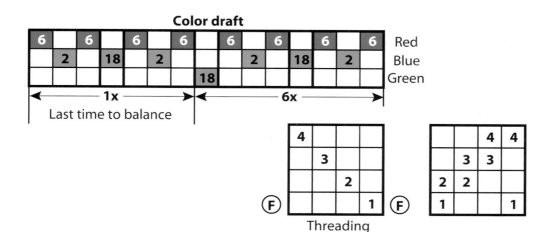

Red
Blue
Green

← 1x → ← 6x →

Last time to balance

Threading

4-SHAFT TWILL

Warp: 2/8 Jagger Spun Merino Wool

Colors:

- Emerald, 108 ends
- Royal, 154 ends
- Garnet, 168 ends

Sett: 12 epi

Width in reed: 38.8"

Warp length: 2.5 yds.

Weft: Same as warp

Note: Beat carefully to weave each color to square. Weave colors in "Tromp as Writ" order.

Hem — 2x, 3x

Body of blanket

Hem — 3x, 2x

Berry Blanket

With a broken twill threading you are unable to weave a true plain weave because of the transitional break between the pattern blocks. The breaks happen when the threading goes from shaft 4 to shaft 2, and again when your threading goes from shaft 3 to shaft 1. A plain weave treadling that alternates the odd shafts with the even numbered shafts produce warp-way stripes of pairs of threads. Take a look at the treadling for the hem of this blanket. It is purposely woven as a twill so that when you roll and sew the hem the twill lines in the pattern run in the same direction as the rest of the pattern. Use a plain weave hem if you prefer.

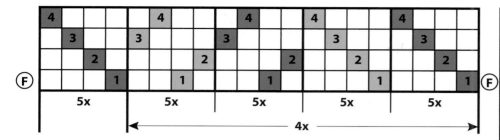

BERRY BLANKET

4-SHAFT DORNICK TWILL CHECK

Warp: Kraemer Yarns
Colors:

Tatamy Tweed, Loganberry, 180 ends

Little Lehigh, Peek-a-Boo, 160 ends

Sett: 10 epi

Width in reed: 34"

Warp length: 2.5 yds.

Weft: Same as warp

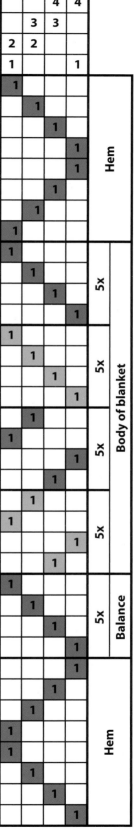

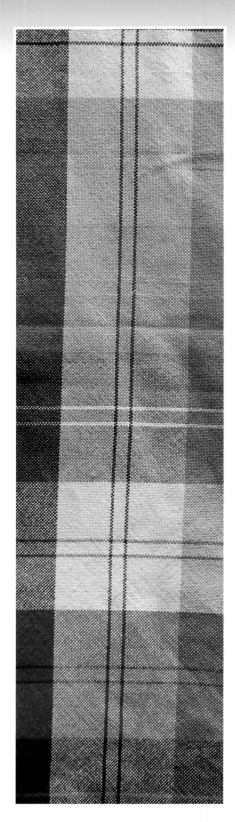

Down the Garden Path

My good friend Sandy showed me a dish towel that she had woven using 8/2 cotton in colors that were inspired by the vegetables from her garden. She had red and golden beets, tomatoes, cucumbers, and many other colorful veggies. What a brilliant idea for a kitchen towel, I thought. And then it struck me that by simply changing the proportions of the color blocks and making the warp wider, this same fabric would make a very nice baby blanket. Sandy wove this blanket.

DOWN THE GARDEN PATH

4-SHAFT PLAIN WEAVE

Warp: 8/2 cotton
  Colors: As listed and amounts on chart

Sett: 20 epi

Width in reed: 33.6"

Warp length: 2.5 yds.

Weft: Same as warp

Note: Starting with mauve, weave the color order "Tromp as Writ," and then reverse back. Weave A, B, C, D, E, F, G, H, G, F, E, D, C, B, A.

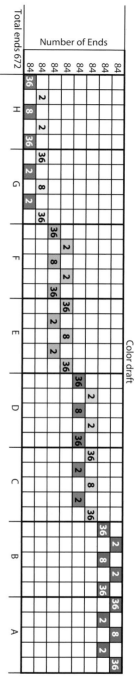

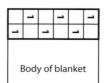

Hem

Body of blanket

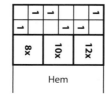

Hem

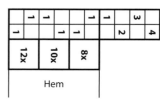

Up the Cherry Tree

This log cabin weave is one of my all-time favorite patterns. It is simply a color and weave effect done with plain weave. I pushed the pattern just a little: I chose colors with strong contrast and used contrasting weights of yarn (by doubling one of the warp colors and using this doubled thread as if it were one). I doubled the opposite color in the weft direction. Tip: Wind two threads together on a bobbin or use a boat shuttle that will accommodate two bobbins and count the number of turns it takes to fill the bobbin. Then wind the same number of turns on the second bobbin. This way they end at just about the same place, which makes it easier to splice in a new bobbin. The heavy/light contrast makes this log cabin pattern look almost three dimensional.

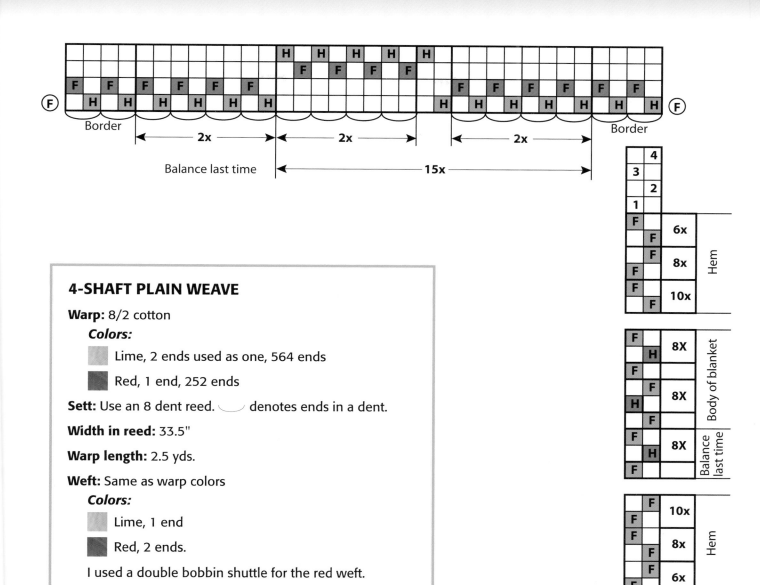

Border | 2x | 2x | 2x | Border

Balance last time | 15x

	4
3	
	2
1	

F		
	F	6x
	F	
F		8x
F		
	F	10x

F		
	H	8X
F		
	F	8X
H		
	F	
F		8X
	H	
F		

Body of blanket / Balance last time

	F	10x
F		
F		8x
	F	
	F	6x
F		

Hem

4-SHAFT PLAIN WEAVE

Warp: 8/2 cotton

Colors:

Lime, 2 ends used as one, 564 ends

Red, 1 end, 252 ends

Sett: Use an 8 dent reed. ⌣ denotes ends in a dent.

Width in reed: 33.5"

Warp length: 2.5 yds.

Weft: Same as warp colors

Colors:

Lime, 1 end

Red, 2 ends.

I used a double bobbin shuttle for the red weft.

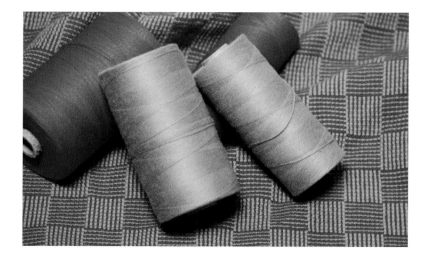

UP THE CHERRY TREE

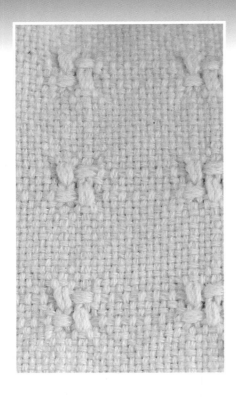

Wynken, Blynken, and Nod

The poem by Eugene Field inspired this canvas weave blanket. (Don't you think a sail for a wooden shoe would be made of canvas?) Canvas weave is great for dish towels because it gives a subtle texture to the fabric, which is also ideal for embroidery. In honor of Jewish tradition, the crocheted edge and the cross-stitched Hebrew letters are blue. And blue is the perfect connection to my blanket and its name. "Wynken, Blynken, and Nod one night sailed off in a wooden shoe; sailed off on a river of crystal light into a sea of BLUE dew."

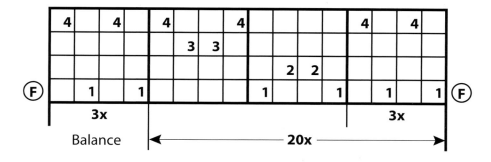

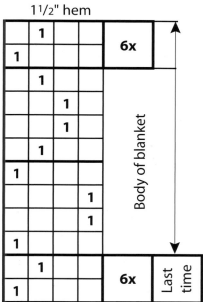

1¹/₂" hem

Body of blanket

WYNKEN, BLYNKEN, AND NOD

4-SHAFT
CANVAS WEAVE

Warp: 8/4 cotton carpet warp

  Color:

  Natural, 412 ends

Sett: 12 epi

Width in reed: 34.3"

Warp length: 2.5 yds.

Weft: 8/4 cotton, same as warp

Note: 5/2 Perle cotton was used to crochet an edge and to cross stitch the baby's name in Hebrew.

Huckleberry Huck

Remember the cartoon character Huckleberry Hound? He was a big blue dog and I just loved him. I wanted to be sure that a book about baby blankets included a pattern using huck lace. Like canvas weave, huck lace is usually woven using just one color thread for both warp and weft. But I just can't seem to leave well enough alone, so in honor of Huckleberry Hound, I included a little color and weave theory into my baby blankets. The result is huck lace with color and texture and a whole lot of interesting things going on. Cheers to Huckleberry Hound, and thanks for the memories!

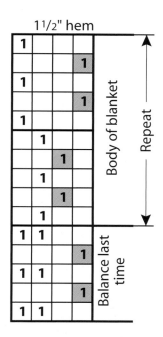

HUCKLEBERRY HUCK

4-SHAFT HUCK LACE

Warp: 8/2 cotton, 655 total ends

Colors:

Alabaster, 258 ends

Nautical Blue, 397 ends

Sett: 20 epi

Width in reed: 32.75"

Warp length: 2.5 yds.

Weft: 8/2 cotton, same as warp

1½" hem

Body of blanket · Repeat

Balance last time

Sweet as a Grape on the Vine

Purple and lime green together? It was almost painful for this old conservative scholar of antique fabrics and rugs. But this book is all about weaving baby blankets, not reproducing the fabrics of our colonial past. And let's face it folks, if years ago people had their hands on aniline dyes, our weaving history would have been changed drastically. These bright colors and this bold twill pattern work well together. If you notice a tiny finger following the diagonal line of this twill, you might just be in the presence of a future weaver.

SWEET AS A GRAPE ON THE VINE

4-SHAFT TWILL

Warp: 8/2 cotton
Colors:

Purple, 424 ends

Pale Lime, 276 ends

Sett: 20 epi

Width in reed: 35"

Warp length: 2.5 yds.

Weft: 8/2 cotton, same as warp

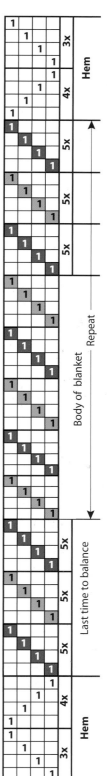

Fortune Cookie

I love Chinese food. And I love spending time in Chinese restaurants decorated to make you believe that you're right there in China. A huge fish tank, maybe a dragon on the wall, and of course a rickshaw converted into a salad bar right in the middle of the restaurant. There are a few color combinations that just say China to me, like the combination of gold, black, and lacquer red. This overshot pattern is sometime referred to as a patch pattern. I have taken what is thought of as a coverlet pattern, reduced the size of the pattern blocks to make them more in scale with a baby blanket, and then used the colors gold, black, and red to convey the feeling of a familiar Chinese sweet.

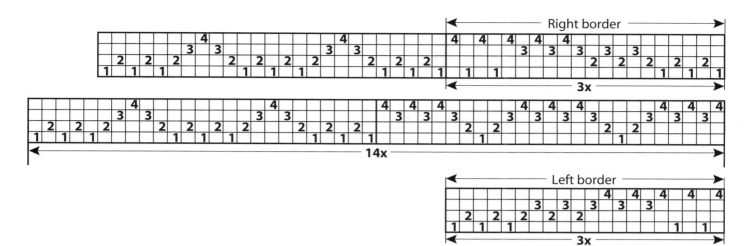

FORTUNE COOKIE

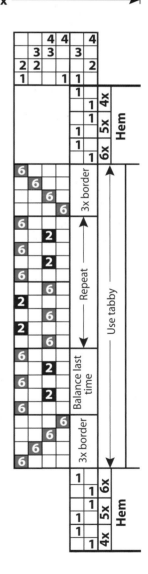

4-SHAFT OVERSHOT

Warp: 10/2 Perle cotton, 845 total ends
   Color:
    California Gold

Sett: 24 epi

Width in reed: 35"

Warp length: 2.5 yds.

Weft: 10/2 cotton for tabby
   Color:
    California Gold

Pattern: 5/2 Perle cotton
   Color:
    Red Hot [color square]
    Black [color square]

Note: Weave tabby hems in California Gold.

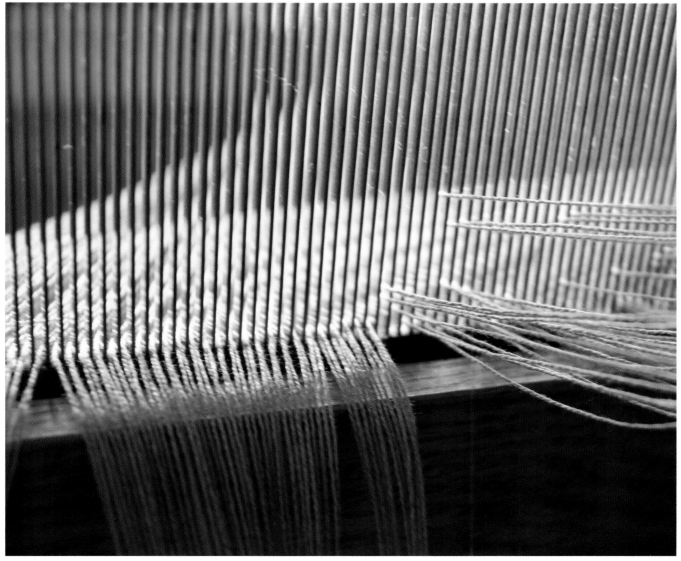

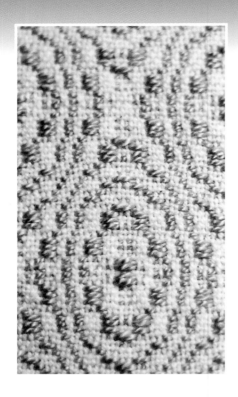

Stars and Roses

I love overshot and even after weaving all these years it still keeps my interest. This is a favorite coverlet pattern. I reduced the scale of the pattern to make it work better for a baby blanket. Here are a few things to remember: it is a two shuttle weave. One shuttle carries your pattern thread and follows the treadling order under the twill columns. The second shuttle carries a finer weight thread than the pattern thread, which allows the pattern thread on the first shuttle to be the dominate thread. The second shuttle weaves tabby, following the throw of the pattern shuttle. Overshot treadlings are shown with only the pattern order. There will be a simple notation that says USE TABBY. This eliminates having such a long treadling sequence. The tabbys produce a plain weave ground fabric below all the decorative pattern rows of the overshot pattern.

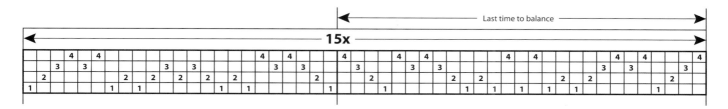

STARS AND ROSES

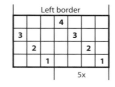

Left border 5x

Right border 6x

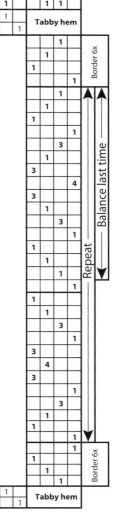

4-SHAFT OVERSHOT

Warp: 10/2 cotton, 824 total ends

   Colors:

     Natural

Sett: 24 epi

Width in reed: 34.4"

Warp length: 2.5 yds.

Weft:

   Pattern:

     5/2 cotton, Jade

   Tabby:

     16/2 cotton, natural

Note: Weave tabby hems.

Fit for Queen or King

The textured yarn that creates the over check is called Queen Anne's Lace from Henry's Attic and is easily available. This blanket is as simple and straightforward as it gets. The colors are gender neutral and although they could stand alone and work as a pretty check fabric, introducing the textured thread adds interest. If constantly changing weft threads is daunting, then consider this: the warp is beautiful with its colored stripes. So why not just use one of the colors from the warp as the weft? Green is gender neutral, fuchsia works for a little girl, and the blue works for a boy. Queen Anne's Lace thread is put up on one pound cones or half pound skeins; you are only using a little bit in the warp so you will have plenty to use alone as the weft to give you a fabulous overall textured blanket. Lots and lots of possibilities—why not make the warp longer and weave several blankets?

FIT FOR QUEEN OR KING

8x balance — **11x** — **8x**

4-SHAFT PLAIN WEAVE

Warp: 8/2 cotton. 560 total ends

Colors:

- Nile, 384 ends
- Blue, 88 ends
- Fuchsia, 44 ends
- Textured cotton Queen Anne's Lace, 44 ends

Sett: 16 epi

Width in reed: 35"

Warp length: 2.5 yds.

Weft: Same as warp

Treadling:
- 4x — Hem
- 5x — Hem
- 16x — Repeat
- 2x
- 1x
- 2x
- 1x
- 2x
- 16x — Balance last time
- 5x — Hem
- 4x — Hem

Goosey Gander's Eye and Goosey Gander's Chevron

Shadow weave is based in twill. Look at the threading draft and follow the threads marked as dark. Can you see how it resembles a point twill? The light threads act as a sort of shadow and play a huge role in the structure. Goosey Gander's Eye uses two colors in the warp and the same two colors in the weft. For the best results, use colors with a strong contrast. For a softer look use two colors that are closer in value. Usually the same colors are used in the weft direction, but of course it doesn't have to be woven that way. In one blanket, Moody Blue was used in both the warp and weft with Parakeet as the shadow. In the second blanket, the strong contrasting color Cranberry was paired with Moody Blue in the weft to make the chevron design really pop.

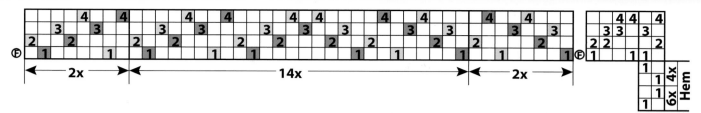

Blanket #1: Goosey Gander's Eye
Tie Up

GOOSEY GANDER'S EYE

4-SHAFT SHADOW WEAVE

Warp: 8/4 cotton carpet warp, 396 total ends

Colors:

Moody Blue, 198 ends

Parakeet, 198 ends

Sett: 12 epi

Width in reed: 33"

Warp length:
2.5 yds. for one blanket
4 yds. for two blankets

Weft: Same as warp

GOOSEY GANDER'S CHEVRON

4-SHAFT SHADOW WEAVE

Warp: 8/4 cotton carpet warp, 396 total ends

Colors:

Moody Blue, 198 ends

Parakeet, 198 ends

Sett: 12 epi

Width in reed: 33"

Warp length:
2.5 yds. for one blanket
4 yds. for two blankets

Weft: Same as warp

Colors:

Moody Blue

Cranberry

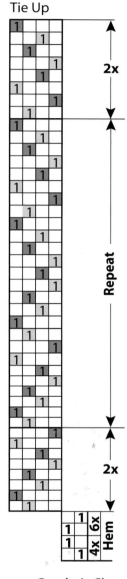

Blanket #1: Goosey Gander's Eye Tie Up

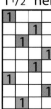

Blanket #2: Goosey Gander's Chevron
Tie Up
1¹/₂" hem in dark blue

1¹/₂" hem in dark blue

Rainbow

This colorful blanket is welcoming and cheery. The warp colors are varying widths to create a random look. The weft is woven with a brightly colored and variegated thread that pulls the whole design together and softens the bold warp stripes. The weft yarn is thick and thin, with slubs. The slubs add interest to the finished fabric but make it impossible to achieve a smooth selvedge edge. I serged the raw warp ends to secure them and then added a single crochet edge on all four sides using a color from the warp. If you like the way the selvedges look and don't want to be bothered with the crocheted edge, simply roll a hem or attach a satin binding

RAINBOW threading draft — shafts 4, 3, 2, 1

3x	6x	3x	3x	6x	3x	3x	6x	3x

Repeat: 4, 3, 2, 1 / 1, 1 — Repeat to desired length

RAINBOW

4-SHAFT PLAIN WEAVE

Warp: Weekend Cotton by Stanley Berroco

Colors:

Iris, 96 ends

Tomatillo, 96 ends

Marigold, 96 ends

Sett: 8 epi

Width in reed: 36"

Warp length: 2.5 yds.

Weft: Florafil, by Made in America

Note: Finish with single crochet or picot crochet edge as you wish.

Rose Garden

This blanket is threaded to a Rose Path twill and I incorporated a design effect known as color and weave. The warp is made up of two contrasting colors that alternate in the threading. Winding the warp is easy because you can wind the two ends together in your hand. The cross will be a two-thread by two-thread cross instead of the usual thread-by-thread cross. Alternating colors helps you keep track of your threading and sleying the reed. The treadling is standard rose path treadling using alternating colors. Plan to use floating selvedges. My blanket shows two colors in the warp and the same two colors in the weft. Why not change one of the colors and exchange it with a different color for the weft? For instance, trade out the cranberry in the warp for navy blue in the weft. Then you will have cranberry and lavender in the warp direction and navy and lavender in the weft direction. The result will be striking.

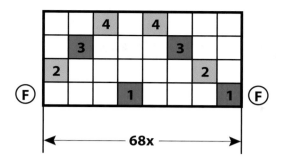

ROSE GARDEN

4-SHAFT ROSE PATH TWILL

Warp: 8/4 cotton carpet warp
Colors:

  Cranberry

  Lavender

Sett: 16 epi

Width in reed: 34"

Warp length: 2.5 yds.

Weft: Same as warp

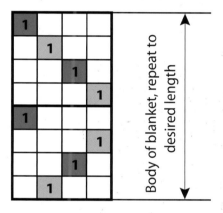

Diamonds in the Sky

ere I have taken another lace weave and combined it with color and weave effects to create a striking fabric. It is beautiful to look at and a whole lot of fun to weave. The alternating colors of blue and stone in the warp and weft create warp-way floats of pale grey on one side of the blanket and weft floats of blue on the other side. Be sure to count your heddles on harness #1 before you get started: every other thread is threaded on harness #1. So with a warp of 532 total ends, half of the warp ends, 266, will be threaded on the first harness and the other 266 threads will be threaded over the other harnesses.

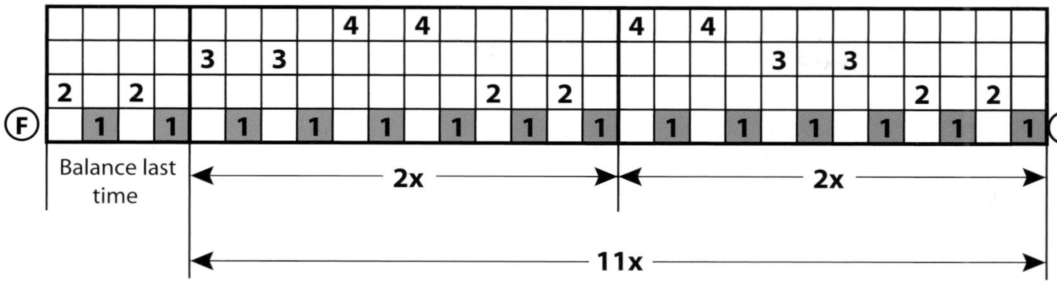
Balance last time
2x
2x
11x

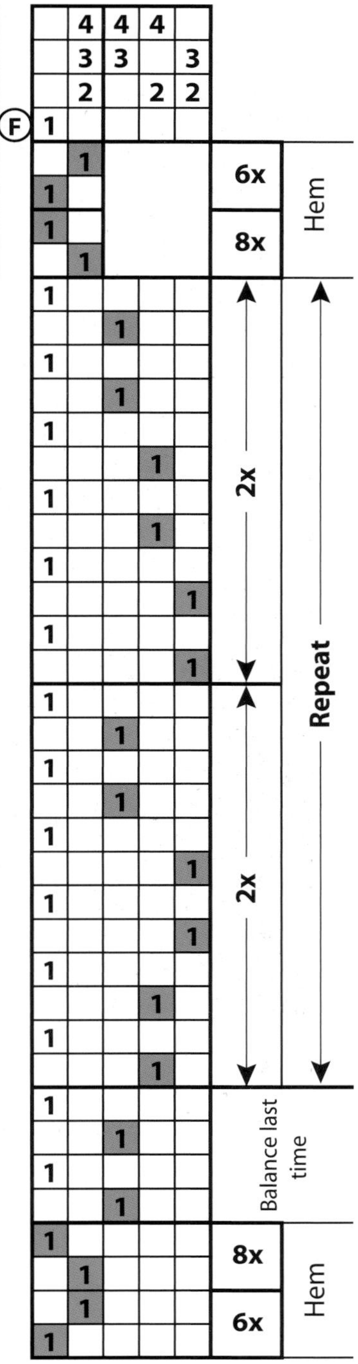
6x
8x
Hem
2x
2x
Repeat
Balance last time
8x
6x
Hem

DIAMONDS IN THE SKY

4-SHAFT SPOT BRONSON

Warp: 5/2 Perle cotton, 532 total ends

Colors:

Nassau, 266 ends

Stone, 266 ends

Sett: 16 epi

Width in reed: 33.25"

Warp length: 2.5 yds.

Weft: Same as warp

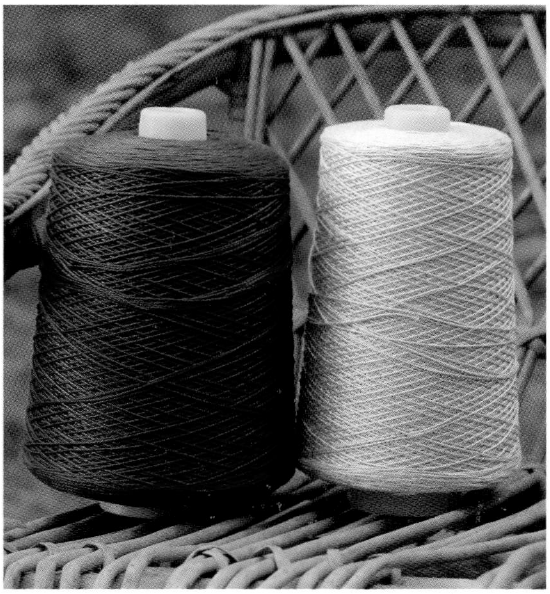

sherbet

So soft and silky—this blanket is woven with a type of rayon thread called Tencel. It has the same properties as rayon so it drapes well. Many weavers use Tencel for scarves and shawls and wearables. The threads used for the baby blanket were hand dyed by two talented women, Cathey Chung and Diane Smith, who call their company JOY (Just Our Yarn). The interplay between the variegated yarn and the bird's eye twill pattern makes a colorful fabric that's so interesting to look at and study. After weaving and hemming, wash it in warm water and a warm rinse. Then put it in the dryer on low heat or air fluff to dry. The change in the finished hand of the fabric is remarkable. You might find it hard to give away, so weave two and keep one for yourself to use as a lap throw.

SHERBET

4-SHAFT BIRD'S EYE TWILL

Warp: 10/2 Tencel, 988 total ends, Joy Yarn
  Colors: Variegated, "Just Our Yarn"

Sett: 30 epi

Width in reed: 33"

Warp length: 2.5 yds.

Weft: Same as warp

Threading draft

Section	Repeat
First block	8x
Middle block	154x
Last block	8x

Threading (shafts 1–4), read with F (selvedge) markers.

Treadling draft (right side):

- Hem — 8x, 10x
- Border — 8x
- Repeat for body of blanket
- Border — 8x
- Hem — 10x, 8x

Summer and Winter Blocks

his weave structure earns its name because the pattern area on one side of the fabric is reversed on the other side. Summer and winter patterns tend to be blocky and crisp. This sharp and graphic pattern reminds me of stacks of wooden baby blocks. The weave structure is a good choice because the surface floats are short and make a tightly woven fabric. Little fingers will find it very difficult to pull out the pattern threads. This particular pattern requires eight harnesses, but there are lots of summer and winter patterns for 4-shaft looms.

Profile draft

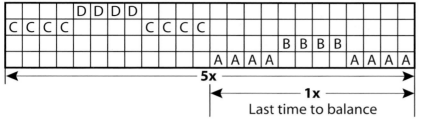

5x

1x

Last time to balance

Key to threading pattern blocks

D		C		B		A	
6	6						
		5	5				
				4	4		
						3	3
	2		2		2		2
		1		1		1		1

SUMMER AND WINTER BLOCKS

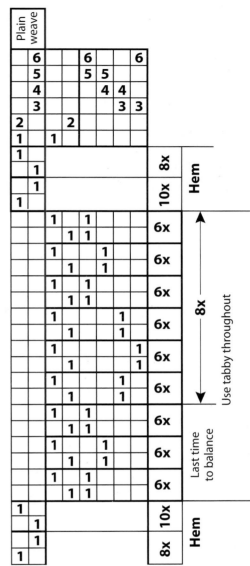

8-SHAFT SUMMER AND WINTER

Warp: 8/2 variegated cotton, 528 ends

Sett: 16 epi

Width in reed: 33"

Warp length: 2.5 yds.

Weft:

Pattern weft: 3/2 Pearle cotton. Magenta or purple
Tabby weft: 8/2 variegated cotton, same as warp

Citrus Drop

What a bright and cheerful blanket. The distinguishing characteristics of this turned twill weave is seen in the two pattern blocks. While one of the pattern blocks is weaving as a warp-emphasis right-leaning twill, the other block is weaving as a weft-emphasis left-leaning twill. To create this pattern, I changed the tie-up from the normal turned twill tie-up to weave solid horizontal bands of weft-emphasis twill. The overall design has cross-hatching lines that resemble a window in a Craftsmen style door. This color combination of yellow and grass green was out of my comfort zone, but it certainly works. Try your own favorite colors, but be sure there is enough contrast in your colors for a wonderful bold and graphic baby blanket.

CITRUS DROP

8-SHAFT TURNED TWILL

Warp: 5/2 Perle cotton, 624 total ends
  Color:
  Yellow

Sett: 20 epi

Width in reed: 31.2"

Warp length: 2.5 yds.

Weft: 5/2 Perle cotton
  Color:
  Bali Green

Profile draft of pattern blocks

Key to threading blocks

B block   A block

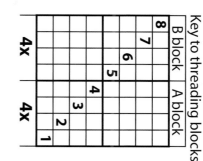

Weaves B blocks

Weaves A blocks

Tie up

Hem

Profile of treadling blocks

Border

Repeat for body of blanket

Border

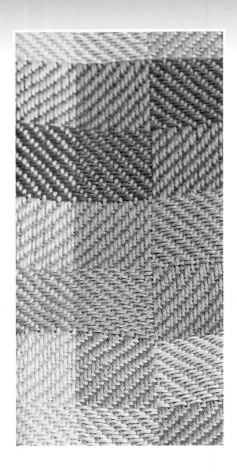

Pink and Blue and Mossy Too

While talking to a woman one day I noticed her interesting jacket. She said it was purchased right off the rack and she bought it because it looked like handwoven material. It was beautiful and I didn't want to miss this opportunity, so I asked her if might keep her for just a few minutes more as I drafted out the pattern. Grabbing my pen, I quickly drafted out a pattern on the back of a scrap receipt in my wallet. Later, as I analyzed my scrap sketch, I realized that the fabric was a variation of a turned twill threading using just two pattern blocks. It was the way the colors were arranged that made this fabric so striking. The pattern reminds me of tumbling wooden baby blocks. I also see pin wheels . . . remember pinwheels? I promise that you will have some fun weaving this pattern—and thinking about pinwheels.

PINK AND BLUE AND MOSSY TOO

8-SHAFT TURNED TWILL

Warp: 5/2 Perle cotton, 720 total ends
Colors:

Petal Pink, 240 ends

Blue Paradise, 240 ends

Avocado Green, 240 ends

Sett: 20 epi

Width in reed: 36"

Warp length: 2.5 yds.

Weft: Same as warp

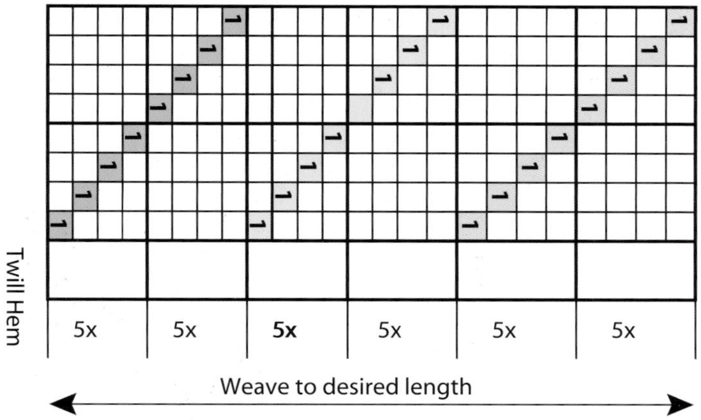

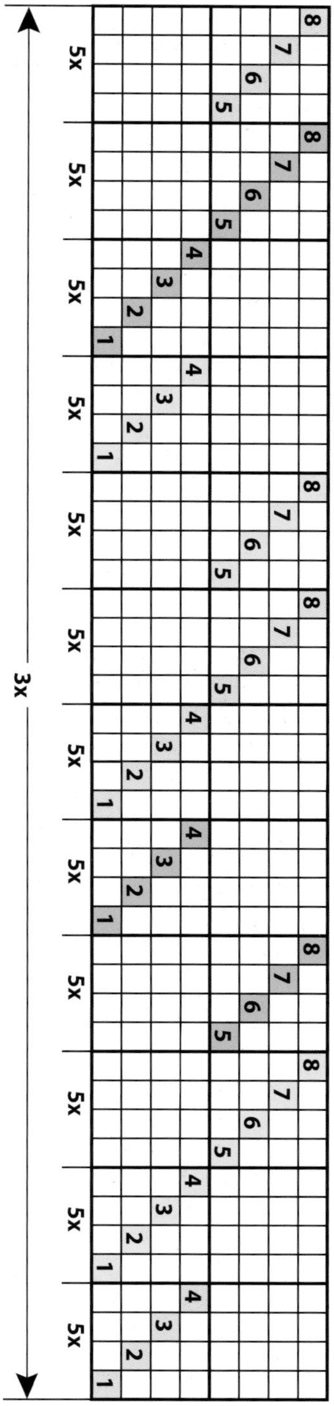

Twill Hem

Twill Hem

5x 5x **5x** 5x 5x 5x

Weave to desired length

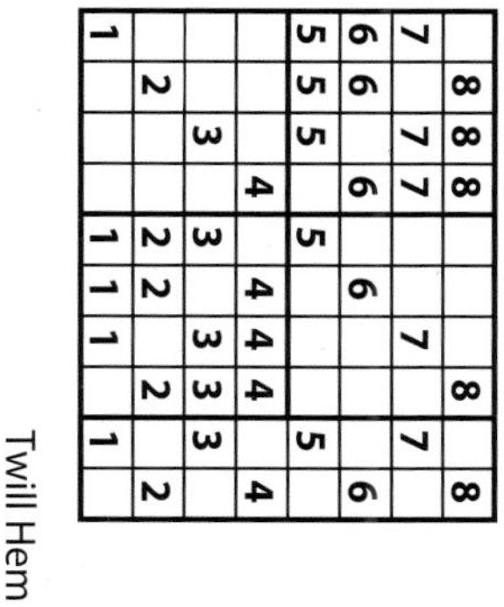

Of Snakes and Snails and Puppy Dog Tails

Y ou couldn't ask for an easier threading pattern than an undulating twill. It is just threaded 1 to 8, again and again. It is the tie-up and the treadling sequence that makes the magic. I used a nice soft cotton for the warp and tabby; the pattern thread is a heavier variegated yarn giving a colorful, soft look. For a bolder effect, use a contrasting solid color for the pattern thread. This is a good choice for a first time 8-harness pattern. The threading is so easy it's hard to get lost and the treadling is similar to weaving a 4-harness overshot pattern, with a pattern thread followed by a tabby thread.

Threading

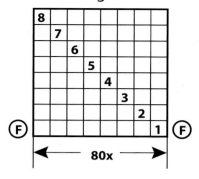

OF SNAKES AND SNAILS AND PUPPY DOG TAILS

8-SHAFT UNDULATING TWILL

Warp: 5/2 Perle cotton, 640 ends
    Colors: Green

Sett: 20 epi

Width in reed: 32"

Warp length: 2.5 yds.

Weft: Same as warp for tabby
    3/2 Variegated cotton for pattern

Note: Weave sections A and B for body of
    blanket. Balance with A section last time.

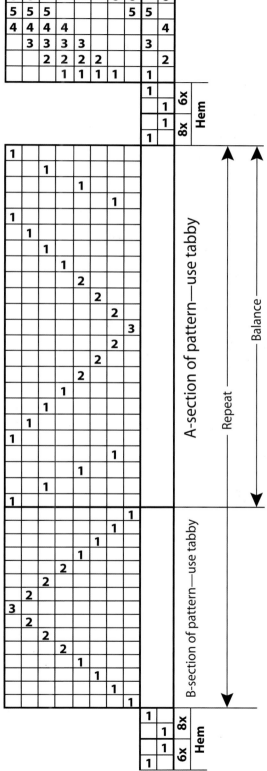

Caramel Corn

The term M's and O's refers to the appearance of the fabric. When you look at this weave structure you will see blocks of plain weave with rounded corners (O's), and pattern blocks of lace that look like the vertical legs of the letter "M". The design has been around for hundreds of years; the antique examples that I have studied are woven in linen. Weave this pattern on 8 shafts and three pattern blocks instead of the usual two that you get on a 4-shaft loom.

Our Little Lamb

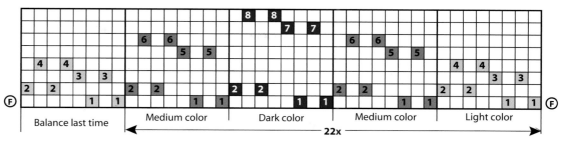

Balance last time | Medium color | Dark color | Medium color | Light color

←—— 22x ——→

CARAMEL CORN

Blanket 1

Blanket 2

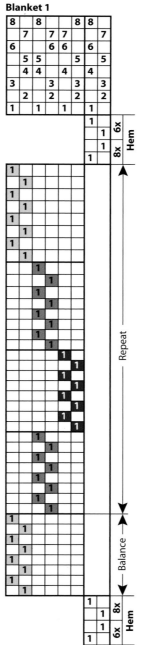

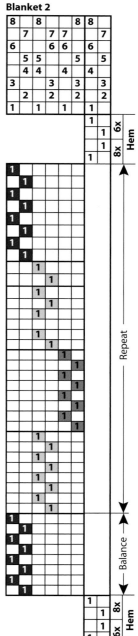

8x · Hem · 6x · Repeat · Balance · 8x · 6x · Hem

8-SHAFT M's AND O's

Warp: 8/2 cotton, 712 ends

Colors:

  Light, 184 ends

  Medium, 352 ends

  Dark, 176 ends

Sett: 20 epi

Width in reed: 35.6"

Warp length: 2.5 yds.

Weft: Same as warp

Sun Spots and Solar Flares

I love a fabric that draws you in and makes you take a closer look. I mean really close. You first look at this blanket and you might say it's pretty. And then you see that there is a whole lot more going on. Huck produces warp floats, or weft floats, or even both warp and weft floats all at the same time, depending on the tie-up of your loom. Huck is a lace weave, and like most lace weaves, it is usually woven using only one color for both the warp and the weft. By using two colors in the warp and the same two colors in the weft a whole new element is added to this classic weave structure. Or try changing out one of the weft colors for a different color. Adding a third color is exciting. How about a warp of pink and blue with wefts of green and yellow? Crazy? Maybe, maybe not. (And look at you becoming a designer!) Weave a sample: if the sample works as you see it in your head, then warp and weave for a blanket. A word of warning folks. This sort of weaving can take you down a path and into an unexpected and unplanned field of study. You might be applying color and weave effects to all sorts of structures. Let me know what you think. I love it and I bet you will too.

SUN SPOTS AND SOLAR FLARES

8-SHAFT HUCK LACE WITH COLOR AND WEAVE EFFECTS

Warp: 5/2 Perle cotton, 565 total ends

Colors:

Red, 343 ends [color square]

Gold, 222 ends [color square]

Sett: 16 epi

Width in reed: 35.3"

Warp length: 2.5 yds.

Weft: Same as warp

Note: Weave pattern blocks in this order: A, B, C, D, E, F, E, D, C, B. Repeat and end with Block A last time. Weave ending hem.

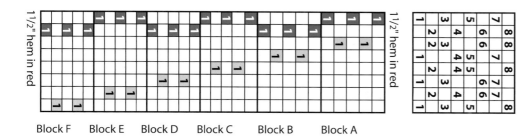

Block F   Block E   Block D   Block C   Block B   Block A

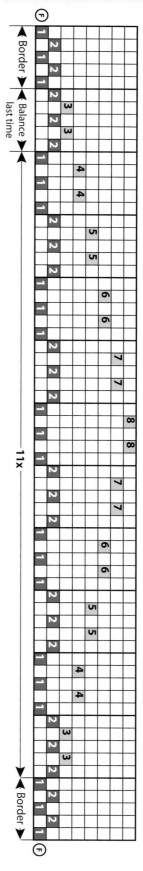

Christening Blanket

There is nothing more beautiful than a family coming together in celebration of a new life. A simple white blanket makes an ideal christening gift for someone new and innocent to life's journey. A white warp and a white weft is difficult when weaving plain weave. Twills are another story. Sometimes it is hard to see if your beat is off or if you made a treadling error. Just knowing that this blanket would be a challenge, I warped with a white 8/2 unmercerized cotton that has a natural mat finish, and wove with a shiny 8/2 rayon thread. This helped me see the pattern develop and prevent mistakes. It worked perfectly. It's a beautiful blanket, perfect for a special baby on a special day.

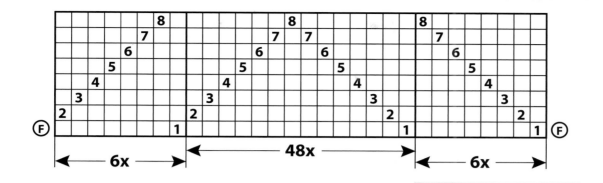

CHRISTENING BLANKET

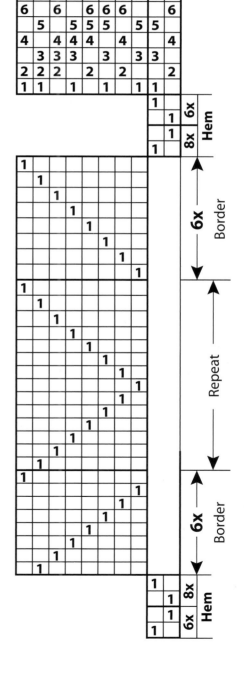

8-SHAFT TWILL

Warp: 8/2 cotton, white, 768 total ends

Sett: 24 epi

Width in reed: 32"

Warp length: 2.5 yds.

Weft: 8/2 rayon, white

Windsor's Blanket

I designed and wove this very special blanket for Windsor, my first grand-daughter. I suppose I don't have to tell many of you out there what a wonder-ful thing it is to be a grandparent. I wanted this to be the best blanket I ever wove, an heirloom for all time. Someday she would sit down as an old woman and tell her own great granddaughter how her grandfather wove this blanket, just for her, with love. And love her I do—because this is the second baby blanket I wove for her! I wove the entire blanket and washed and finished it and didn't once see a threading error caught by one of my eagle-eyed students. So back to the loom again to weave another blanket for my Windsor. This one would be perfect.

8-SHAFT ADVANCING TWILL

Warp: 5/2 Perle cotton, 603 total ends
  Colors:
  ▨ Melon

Sett: 20 epi

Width in reed: 31"

Warp length: 2.5 yds.

Weft: 5/2 Perle cotton
  Colors:
  ▨ Ruby Glint
  Tabby: 10/2 Perle cotton
  ▨ Melon

Note: Weave hem and beginning border, then weave A to E for the body. Weave A to B for balance, ending border. Weave the hem. Use tabby throughout.

WINDSOR'S BLANKET

KEY TO THREADING	
Right border	32
A–E 5x	500
A–B 1x	39
Left border	32
	603

Threading, below
(Tie-up and treadling on page 80)

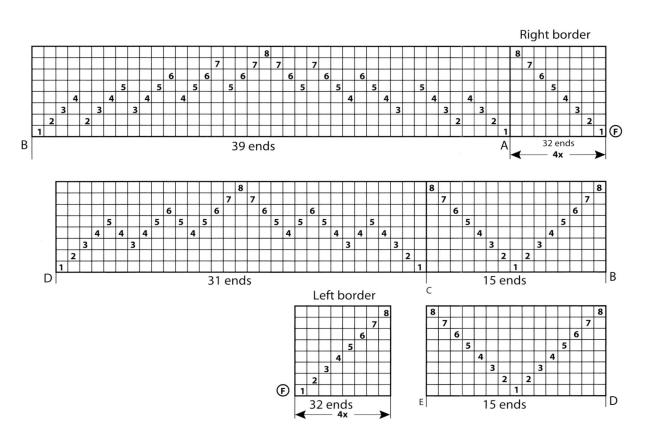

Right border

B — 39 ends — A — 32 ends 4x — (F)

D — 31 ends — C — 15 ends — B

Left border

(F) — 32 ends 4x —

E — 15 ends — D

WINDSOR'S BLANKET

(Tie-up and treadling)

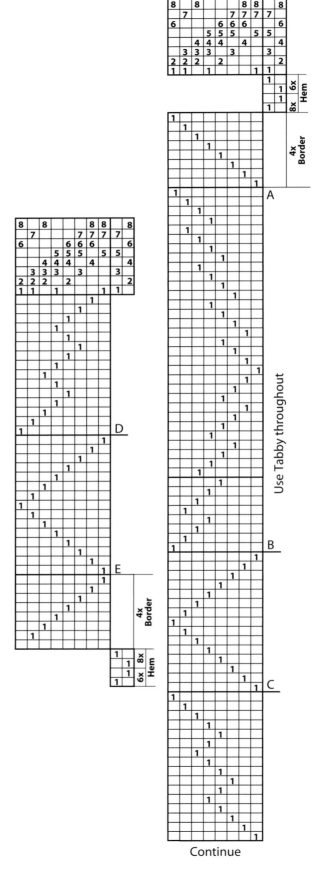

4x Border

8x Hem

6x

A

Use Tabby throughout

B

C

Continue

D

E

4x Border

6x 8x Hem

It's A Boy!

This marvelous checkerboard pattern alternates blocks of plain weave with basket weave. A soft blue DK weight yarn, a cotton and acrylic blend named "It's a Boy!" is perfect for a baby blanket. Often used to knit baby clothing, the properties of this yarn make it wonderful for a blanket.

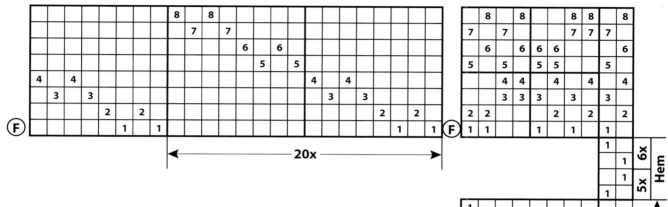

IT'S A BOY!

8-SHAFT BASKET WEAVE

Warp: Tatamy Tweed, DK weight, 328 ends
  Color: L20929, "It's a Boy"

Sett: 10 EPI

Width in reed: 33"

Warp length: 2.5 yds.

Weft: Same as warp

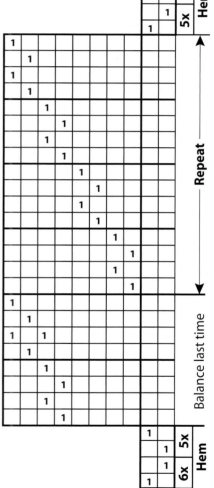

For William or Mary

*T*his is a very old pattern. It gets its name from the threading: can you see how the twill resembles an *M* and the next portion is inverted so it looks like a *W*? I designed this to be woven as a check, the *M*s in one color and the *W*s the other. I would carry this idea into the treadling order and the result is a check pattern with a really interesting pattern within each block of color. This pattern lends itself to so many possibilities: you should wind the warp nice and long so that you can weave several variations. Weave the blanket with just one weft color for vertical stripes. Or the warp could be one color and the weft something different. And like the christening blanket, you could weave white on white or any color with itself.

FOR WILLIAM OR MARY

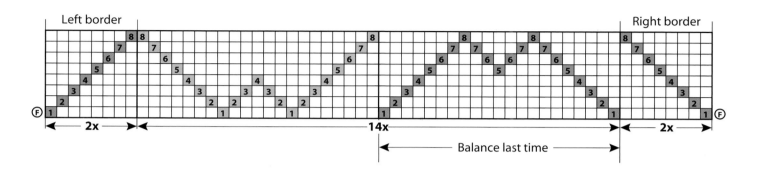

Left border · Right border

2x · 14x · 2x

Balance last time

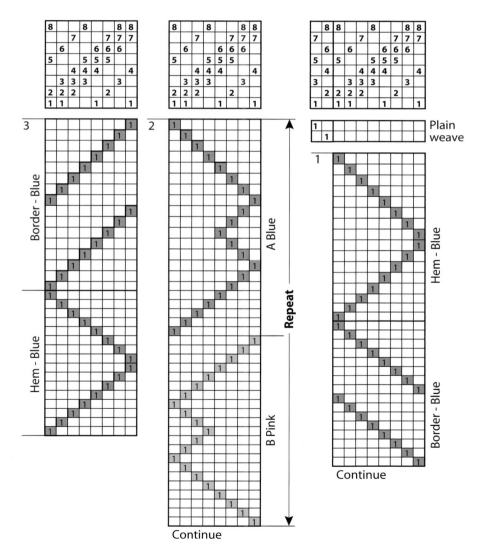

8-SHAFT
M's AND W's TWILL

Warp: 8/2 cotton, 641 total ends

Colors:

Blue, 347 ends

Pink, 294 ends

Sett: 20 epi

Width in reed: 32"

Warp length: 2.5 yds. for one blanket

Weft: same as warp

Note: Weave patterns A and B to desired length and balance with A.

Plain weave

Border - Blue

Hem - Blue

A Blue

Repeat

B Pink

Continue

Hem - Blue

Border - Blue

Continue

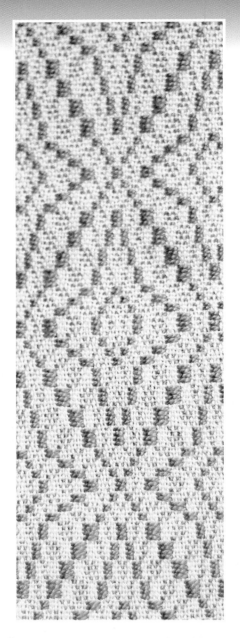

Star of Bethlehem

I took the 4-shaft overshot threading draft and converted it to weave on 8 shafts so that I could play with the tie-up and move the shadowy half tones away from the pattern blocks and make the overall design bolder. The colors used for this blanket are unconventional and they have such a strong contrast that I knew the pattern would pop. The colors don't scream boy or girl—they are neutral. And the reverse side of the blanket is as interesting as the front. You will love weaving the blanket as you watch the pattern blocks grow.

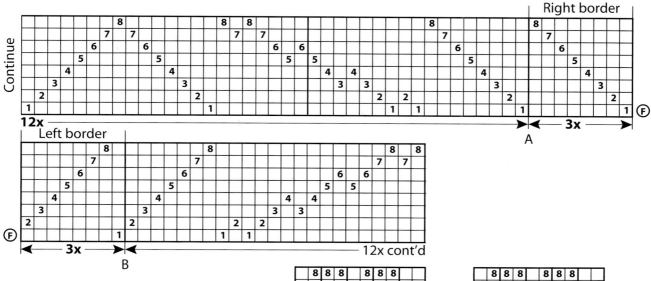

Continue

Right border

12x 3x

A

Left border

F

3x B

12x cont'd

F

STAR OF BETHLEHEM

8-SHAFT OVERSHOT

Warp: 10/2 Perle cotton, 792 total ends. Thread A to B twelve times.

Colors:

Champagne

Sett: 24 epi

Width in reed: 33"

Warp length: 2.5 yds.

Weft:

Pattern:

5/2 Perle cotton, Jade Green

Tabby:

10/2 Pearle cotton, Champagne

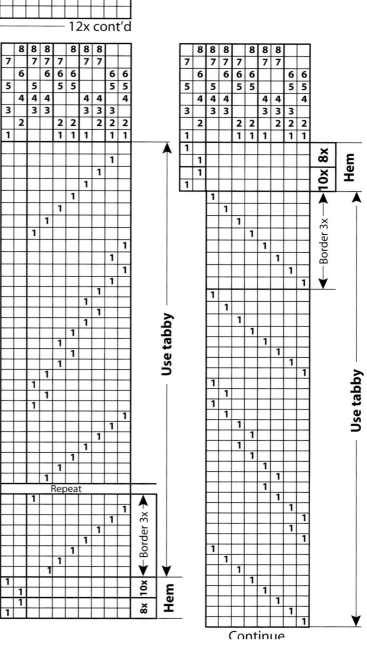

Use tabby

Repeat

Border 3x

8x 10x

Hem

8x 10x

Border 3x

Hem

Use tabby

Continue

Blue Blocks

Double weave makes such a nice soft and warm blanket because it's woven in two layers. With an 8-shaft loom you can weave blocks of pattern of different sizes. The edges of the pattern blocks are connected because the warp and weft threads are exchanged from weaving on the top layer to weaving on the lower layer. Double weave is usually woven with two colors in both the warp and weft. For this blanket I used a variegated thread. The result is a pattern block that resembles ikat. I have also included a tie-up and treadling for a special hem treatment. This will weave two separate layers that can be turned in on themselves, making for a neater hem and reducing the bulk usually found with a traditional rolled hem.

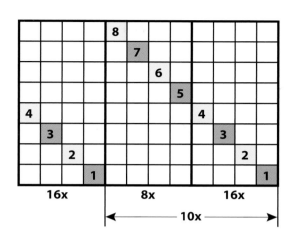

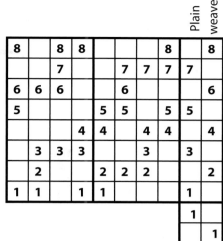

Cross section of blanket & hem

2" beginning hem

2" ending hem

Length of blanket

BLUE BLOCKS

Plain weave

Repeat

16x

8x

Balance

16x

Hem

Top
Bottom
Top
Bottom

8-SHAFT DOUBLE WEAVE

Warp: 8/2 cotton

Colors:

Blue, 512 ends

Variegated, 512 ends

Sett: 32 epi

Width in reed: 32"

Warp length: 2.5 yds.

Weft: Same as warp

Note: For the hem, weave 2": you will be weaving 2 layers. When the blanket is off the loom, turn the ends inward and sew the folded ends together.

Into the Woods

*T*encel is a new generation of rayon. The combination of the Tencel thread and this pretty threading is great fun to weave. An iridescence pops out when these colors are woven together, due to the color interaction and the shine of the thread. So choose your colors carefully: choose two colors with striking contrast of light and color, from warm to cool, for this complex design.

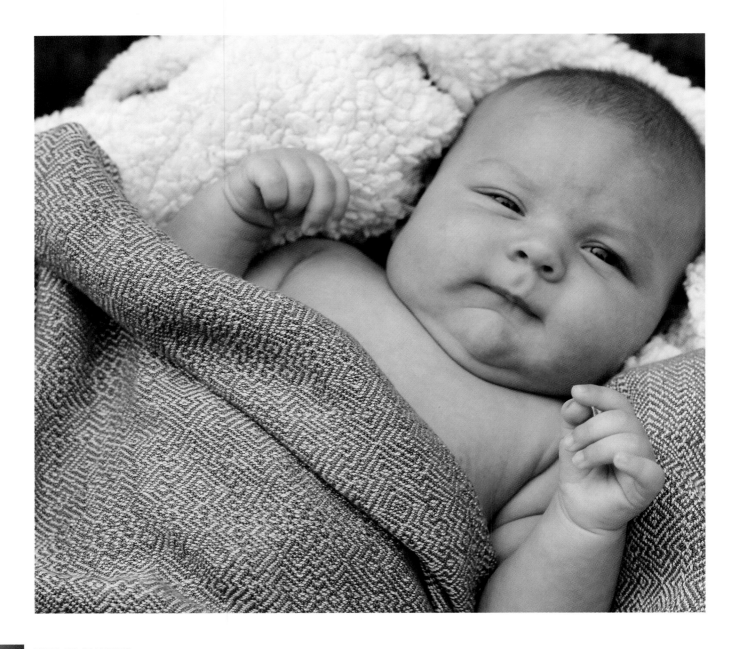

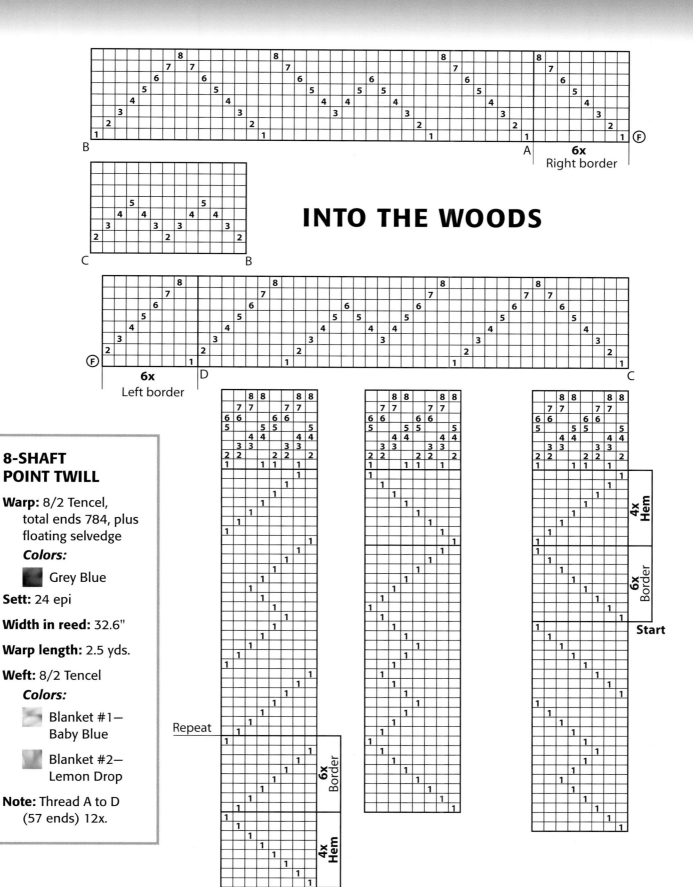

INTO THE WOODS

6x Right border

6x Left border

8-SHAFT POINT TWILL

Warp: 8/2 Tencel, total ends 784, plus floating selvedge

Colors:

■ Grey Blue

Sett: 24 epi

Width in reed: 32.6"

Warp length: 2.5 yds.

Weft: 8/2 Tencel

Colors:

Blanket #1— Baby Blue

Blanket #2— Lemon Drop

Note: Thread A to D (57 ends) 12x.

Repeat

6x Border

4x Hem

4x Hem

6x Border

4x Hem

6x Border

Start

Notes from a Weaver and Photographer of Baby Blankets

It was an honor to help with this book. Tom Knisely is my teacher so at first I was a bit intimidated. While he is a Master Weaver, I considered myself just a beginner. In the 1970s, I got my first old 2-harness Union rug loom from a neighbor's barn. Friends helped me with a few projects, and then I signed up for my first beginning weaving class with Tom. During the week-long class, I decided that I needed a second loom, so I found a used, 4-harness Gallinger. I have the antique 2-harness loom in my living room for plain weave scarves and rugs, while the newer version is upstairs in a cozy weaving nook for the production of items beyond plain tabby. I do a lot of weaving.

In spite of the classes and practice, however, I still felt like a beginner. I picked projects with simplicity in mind because I wanted to be certain I could do them. I have woven almost all of the traditional weave structures but nothing too complicated or with too many threads. If I wove using Tencel at 24 epi, it was for a huck shawl with a simple stripe. My baby blankets for my grandchildren were made with heavy yarn so that it wouldn't take quite as many ends to complete a project 36" wide. When selecting a draft for kitchen towels, I would certainly pick the one with two colors over the one with six.

So it took my breath away when I got the draft for Fortune Cookie, which required 845 threads and three colors. I didn't even have that many heddles! But I took a deep breath, bought some more heddles, dressed the loom ever so carefully, and wove an amazingly beautiful blanket that I never would have chosen to do on my own.

Although I still wouldn't consider myself an accomplished weaver, now I am much more self-assured and would gladly try any weave structure with any yarn and as many threads as it takes. And if I can do it, anyone can do it.

So start at the front of the book and weave them all. Not only will you be ready for baby showers for a long, long time, but you will become a much more accomplished weaver too. If you don't want that many baby blankets, change the projects into table runners or shawls—but try them. And for those of you who are already confident weavers, I suspect

these blanket drafts will inspire you to go even further on your weaving journey.

As for the photography, most of the pictures took hours to achieve and many were the result of multiple photo shoots. I love babies, but they certainly are unpredictable. If I wanted the child to be asleep, he would be wide awake, and vice versa. I have many photos of children with blankets over their heads as well as shots of big brothers and sisters attempting to hold squirmy little ones. Twins were twice the challenge! If one was smiling, the other would be crying and trying to get away. If one twin was looking at the camera, the other had a finger up her nose. I don't think there is one photo in this book that came out as I had planned; nonetheless, it was a delightful process, and it warms my heart to think of the time and effort each family donated to the project. I have learned that it's a lot easier to weave a baby blanket than it is to photograph a baby with a blanket!

Enjoy Tom's book and all the cuddly weaving. I'm sure it will result in a lot of beautiful photos of little ones snuggling with their heirloom blankets—or putting them on their heads!

—Kathleen Eckhaus,
weaver and photographer

Acknowledgments

This book would not have been possible without the help of many of my enthusiastic weaving friends. They would say time and time again, "Please design another baby blanket—give me the yarns and threads and I will weave it for you." And weave they did, making this book possible.

Very special thanks to Kathleen Eckhaus. She planted the seed for this book in my head. I had always planned to weave my granddaughter a blanket but never thought to take it further and develop a book devoted to baby blankets. She is also an accomplished photographer and she used the children from her music classes as models for the book. Trying to get toddlers to cooperate and model blankets became quite the undertaking. Thank you from the bottom of my heart for getting such marvelous photos. You are brilliant.

Thanks also to all the children and their parents who graciously allowed and shared their sweet babies to be photographed for this book.

Thanks to all the other weavers who helped me: Susan Kesler Simpson, Sandy Morales, Careena Emrich, Sara Bixler, Brenda Kuyper, Judith Ciancio, Schelly Reynolds, Cynthia Baker, Amanda Robinette, Vonnie Davis, and Kathy King. Thank you, thank you, thank you.

These are more than my students and family, they are also my friends. They were honest and straightforward and were never afraid to call and ask about a tie-up or sett. A special thank you to Kathy King. After threading a thousand or so heddles to my intended 8-shaft twill, the pattern got lost with the threads that I was promoting. So Kathy said, "How about I just rethread the warp to a simple Rose Path and change the weft thread to another color. Is that all right with you?" What a friend!

Thank you Cathey Chung and Diane Smith from Just Our Yarns for dyeing a special-request Tencel thread for one of the blankets.

Thank you, Debra Smith, my editor, and all the wonderful people at Stackpole Books.

Lastly, thank you to my granddaughter Windsor Bixler. You inspired me to write this book so weavers all over would have a source of patterns to go to and help them weave a blanket for their babies.

Resources

Here are the titles of a few books, DVDs and periodicals you might find helpful on your weaving adventures.

Summer & Winter: A Weave for all Seasons. Donna Sullivan. Interweave Press, 1991

Weaving Overshot: Redesigning the Tradition. Donna Lee Sullivan, Interweave Press, 1996

Learning to Weave. Debra Chandler, Interweave Press, 1995

A Handweavers Pattern Book. Marguerite Porter Davison, 1950

The Complete Book of Drafting for Handweavers. Madelyn van der Hoogt, 1993

Pink and Blue: Telling the Boys from the Girls in America. Jo B. Paoletti, Indiana University Press, 2012

A Handweaver's Pattern Directory. Anne Dixon, Interweave Press, 2008

A Loom Owner's Companion. DVD. Tom Knisely, Interweave Press, 2012

The Weaver's Yarn Companion. DVD. Tom Knisely, Interweave Press, 2014

Weaving Rag Rugs. Tom Knisely, Stackpole Books, 2014

Handwoven magazine. Interweave Press

Visual Index

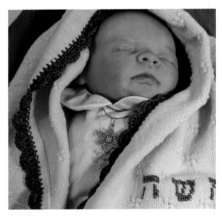

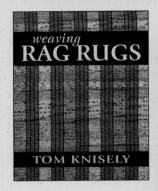
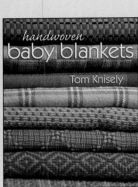

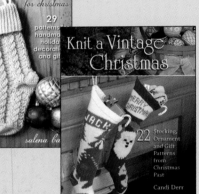